A LOOK AT WORLD HISTORY

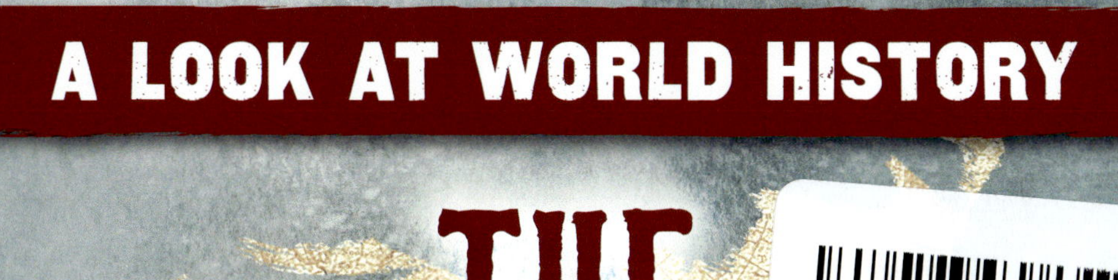

THE RENAISSANCE

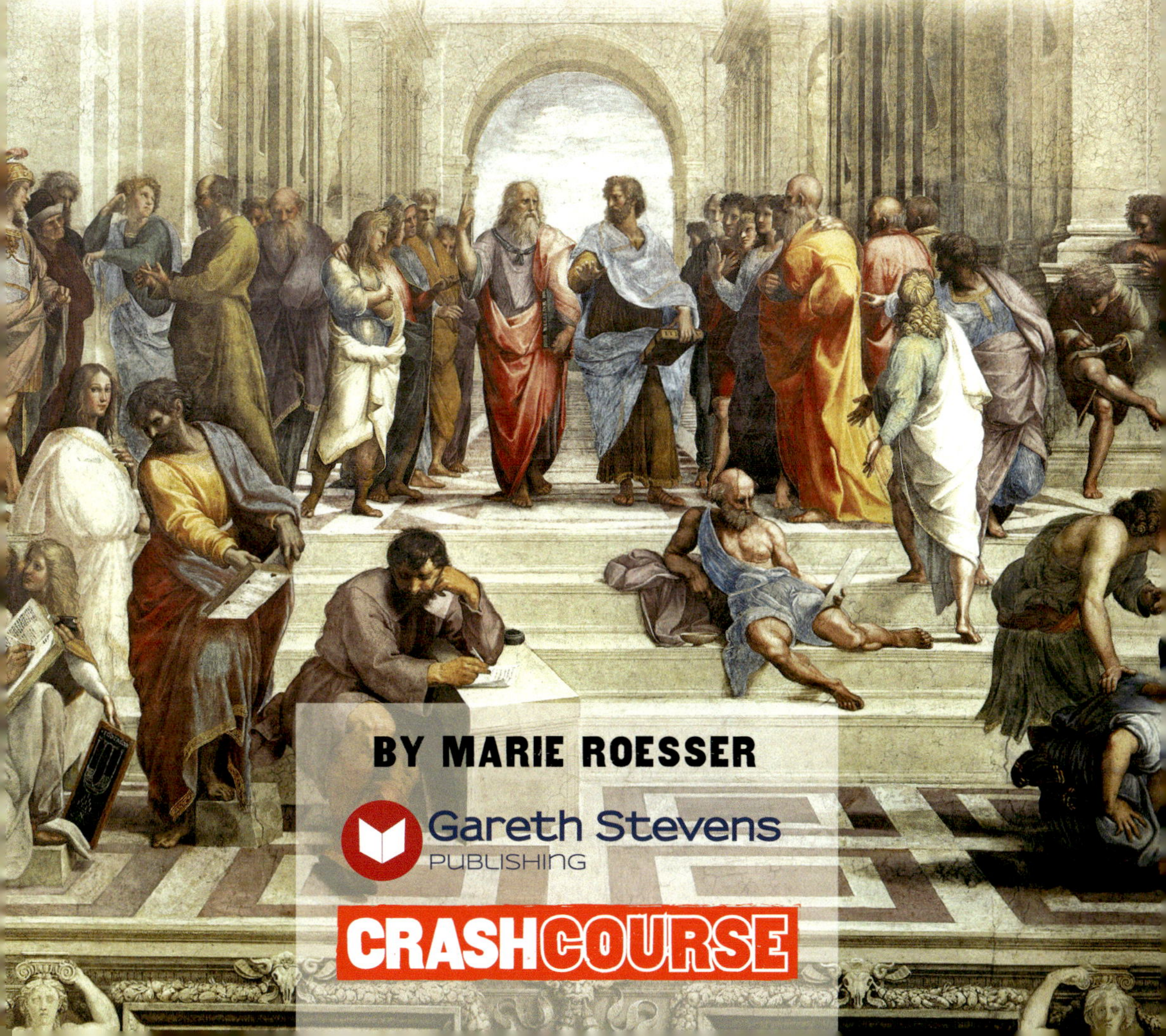

BY MARIE ROESSER

Gareth Stevens Publishing

CRASHCOURSE

Please visit our website, www.garethstevens.com. For a free color catalog of all our high-quality books, call toll free 1-800-542-2595 or fax 1-877-542-2596.

Library of Congress Cataloging-in-Publication Data

Names: Roesser, Marie, author.
Title: The Renaissance / Marie Roesser.
Description: New York : Gareth Stevens Publishing, [2020] | Series: A look at world history | Includes index.
Identifiers: LCCN 2018046480| ISBN 9781538241462 (pbk.) | ISBN 9781538241486 (library bound) | ISBN 9781538241479 (6 pack)
Subjects: LCSH: Renaissance--Juvenile literature.
Classification: LCC CB361 R64 2020 | DDC 940.2/1--dc23
LC record available at https://lccn.loc.gov/2018046480

First Edition

Published in 2020 by
Gareth Stevens Publishing
111 East 14th Street, Suite 349
New York, NY 10003

Designer: Katelyn E. Reynolds
Editor: Therese Shea

Photo credits: Cover, pp. 1, 5 SuperStock/Getty Images; cover, pp. 1–32 (background) javarman/Shutterstock.com; cover, pp. 1–32 (border) Anastasiia Smiian/Shutterstock.com; pp. 7, 25 Bettmann/Getty Images; p. 9 (map) brichuas/Shutterstock.com; p. 9 (inset) The Yorck Project (2002) 10.000 Meisterwerke der Malerei (DVD-ROM), distributed by DIRECTMEDIA Publishing GmbH. ISBN: 3936122202./Hohum/Wikipedia.org; pp. 11, 15 Leemage/Corbis via Getty Images; p. 13 Fine Art Images/Heritage Images/Getty Images; p. 17 (left) Jastrow/Wikipedia.org; p. 17 (right) Sailko/Wikipedia.org; p. 19 (main) website of National Gallery, London (http://www.nationalgallery.org.uk/paintings/jan-van-eyck-the-arnolfini-portrait)/Pimbrils/Wikipedia.org; p. 19 (inset) Bernd vdB/Wikipedia.org; p. 21 TTstudio/Shutterstock.com; p. 23 iryna1/Shutterstock.com; p. 27 Portolanero/Wikipedia.org; p. 29 Alonso de Mendoza/Wikipedia.org.

Printed in the United States of America

CPSIA compliance information: Batch #CS19GS: For further information contact Gareth Stevens, New York, New York at 1-800-542-2595.

CONTENTS

Words in the glossary appear in **bold** type the first time they are used in the text.

A REBIRTH

The Renaissance is the period of European history that followed the Middle Ages. The name is from an old French word that means "rebirth." During the Renaissance, people had new interest in the ideas of the ancient Greeks and Romans.

ANCIENT GREEKS IN THE RENAISSANCE PAINTING *THE SCHOOL OF ATHENS*

MAKE THE GRADE

The Middles Ages lasted from about AD 500 to 1500. However, there's no exact end of the Middle Ages and no exact beginning of the Renaissance.

SOCIETY CHANGES

In the 1300s, a **plague** called the Black Death swept through Europe, killing millions. This led to changes in **society**. People questioned their beliefs, including their **religion**. And people changed their place in communities. Farmers became merchants. Merchants became rich lords.

MAKE THE GRADE

Many rich merchants used their money to become patrons, or supporters, of artists. Art was an important part of the Renaissance.

Towns and cities across Europe grew through the Middle Ages and into the Renaissance. They were centers of trade and **culture**. Florence, in today's Italy, was one of these cities. The Renaissance began there in the 1300s.

MAKE THE GRADE

The Medici family of Florence was one of the most powerful of the Renaissance. They were traders, bankers, and patrons of the arts. Giovanni de' Medici became Pope Leo X in 1513.

HEROES OF HUMANISM

The Italian poet Petrarch was one of the first Renaissance writers. He studied ancient Greek and Roman writings closely. He believed ancient **philosophies** and Christianity were linked. He thought people could learn from both. He began a movement called humanism.

MAKE THE GRADE

Petrarch's most famous poems are about a woman he loved named Laura. No one knows who she really was.

Humanism was the heart of Renaissance thinking. It allowed people to study the world and seek wisdom without **influence** from religious teachings. Humanism wasn't against religion but stated truth and values could be found in all philosophies.

DESIDERIUS ERASMUS

MAKE THE GRADE

Desiderius Erasmus was a Dutch humanist who taught that people shouldn't just practice religion but also try to be good.

Another Renaissance writer who believed in humanism was Giovanni Boccaccio. This Italian man was famous for writing a book of tales called the *Decameron*. He also studied ancient Greek and Roman writings and aided in the search for lost works of ancient writers.

GIOVANNI BOCCACCIO

MAKE THE GRADE

Boccaccio was the first Italian in hundreds of years to learn to read ancient Greek!

RENAISSANCE ART

Just as authors looked to the works of ancient Greeks and Romans, so did artists. Artists of the early Renaissance tried to create the perfect human form. They also closely studied nature and focused less on religious subjects.

DONATELLO

DONATELLO'S STATUE *ST. GEORGE* IN FLORENCE

MAKE THE GRADE

Donatello, who lived from about 1386 to 1466, was a great sculptor of the early Italian Renaissance.

In the 1400s and 1500s, Italian artists Raphael, Leonardo da Vinci, and Michelangelo created great works of art. Jan van Eyck, born in today's Belgium, perfected a new method of oil painting. These artists painted more **realistically** than past artists.

MAKE THE GRADE

Leonardo da Vinci was a sculptor, painter, scientist, **architect**, and inventor. He drew a plan for an early kind of helicopter!

RENAISSANCE ARCHITECTURE

Renaissance architects looked to Greek and Roman buildings when creating new buildings. Renaissance buildings were often symmetrical, which means they looked the same on both sides of a center line. Many were rectangular and had **columns** and **domes**.

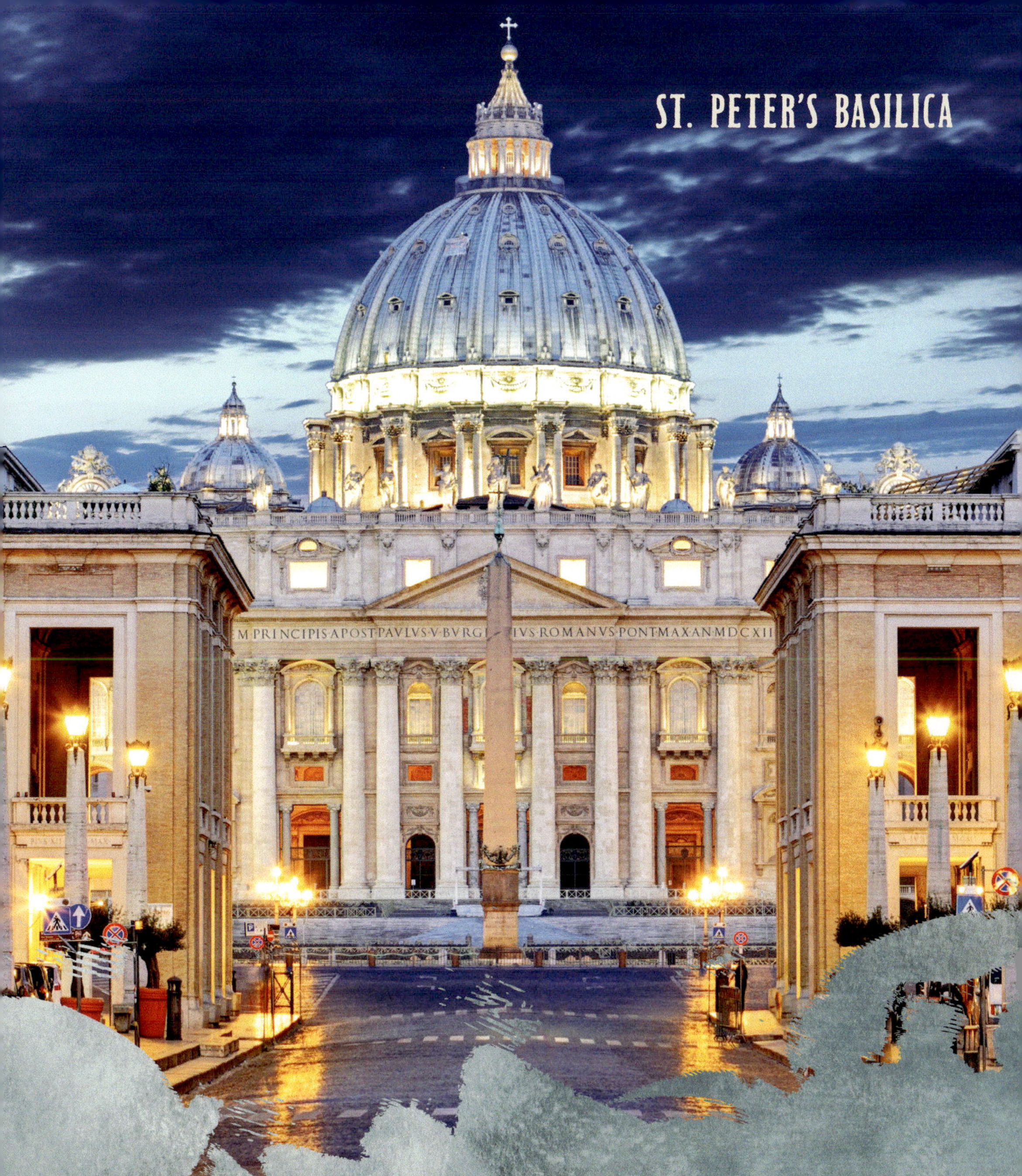

MAKE THE GRADE

St. Peter's Basilica is a large church in Vatican City in Rome, Italy. Completed in the 1600s, it's a great work of Renaissance architecture.

RENAISSANCE SCIENTISTS

Humanism allowed people to question beliefs and test ideas. This led to scientific discoveries. In 1543, Polish scientist Nicolaus Copernicus published a book stating that Earth circled the sun. That opposed what most people mistakenly thought—that the sun went around Earth.

MAKE THE GRADE

The telescope was invented during the Renaissance. Italian scientist Galileo Galilei built his own around 1609 and used it to make discoveries about space.

THE PRINTING PRESS

Certain inventions of the Renaissance also changed ways of life. German Johannes Gutenberg made a kind of printing press around 1440 that allowed books to be printed quickly. More people learned to read, and new ideas spread more easily.

MAKE THE GRADE

Gutenburg didn't invent the printing press with movable type, but he made an improved press. Movable type is blocks with letters on them that can be moved to print different words.

JOURNEYS WEST

In the 1300s, the writings of Ptolemy, an ancient **geographer**, were found. Ptolemy wrote that Europeans could reach India by sailing west. Christopher Columbus read these writings. He tried to find a route to East Asia in 1492. More explorers followed.

MAKE THE GRADE

Columbus landed in the Americas on his journeys west. However, he thought he was in East Asia!

COMING TO AN END

In the late 1400s and 1500s, wars were fought across Italy. People who gave money to artists had less money to support them. In addition, the Catholic Church began to fight against humanism. Slowly, the Renaissance period came to an end.

MAKE THE GRADE

In 1527, soldiers of the Holy Roman Empire destroyed the city of Rome, one of the last centers of Renaissance culture. This, too, helped end the Renaissance.

KEY DATES OF THE RENAISSANCE

1304
Petrarch, one of the founders of humanism, is born.

1347
The Black Death arrives in Europe, killing millions.

1350
Giovanni Boccaccio writes the *Decameron* around this date.

1440
Johannes Gutenberg invents a new kind of printing press.

1492
Christopher Columbus makes his first trip to the Americas.

1503
Leonardo da Vinci begins the *Mona Lisa*.

1504
Michelangelo finishes the sculpture *David*.

1511
Raphael completes *The School of Athens*.

1527
Soldiers of the Holy Roman Empire take over Rome.

1543
Nicolaus Copernicus publishes a book stating that Earth circles the sun.

1609
Galileo makes an improved telescope.

1626
St. Peter's Basilica is completed.

GLOSSARY

architect: a person who designs buildings

column: a tall, strong supporting post

culture: artistic activities such as music, theater, and painting

dome: a rounded roof

geographer: one who studies Earth and its features

Holy Roman Empire: an empire made up of German and Italian territories that existed from the 9th or 10th century to 1806

influence: to have an effect on

philosophy: a system of thought made to try to understand the nature of that which is real

plague: an illness that causes death and that spreads quickly to a large number of people

realistically: in a way that shows people and things as they are in real life

religion: a belief in and way of honoring a god or gods

sculptor: an artist who creates shapes with stone, wood, metal, or other matter

society: the people of a country, area, or time thought of as an organized community

FOR MORE INFORMATION

BOOKS

Fitzpatrick, Anne. *The Renaissance: Movements in Art.* Mankato, MN: Creative Education, 2015.

Marcovitz, Hal. *Life During the Renaissance.* San Diego, CA: ReferencePoint Press, 2016.

WEBSITE

Renaissance for Kids
www.ducksters.com/history/renaissance.php
Learn about people and events of the Renaissance period.

Publisher's note to educators and parents: Our editors have carefully reviewed this website to ensure that it is suitable for students. Many websites change frequently, however, and we cannot guarantee that a site's future contents will continue to meet our high standards of quality and educational value. Be advised that students should be closely supervised whenever they access the internet.

INDEX